A FEW

OBSERVATIONS

ON THE

MODE OF ATTACK,

AND EMPLOYMENT OF THE

HEAVY ARTILLERY

AT

CIUDAD RODRIGO AND BADAJOZ, IN 1812,
AND ST. SEBASTIAN, IN 1813;

WITH

A DISCUSSION ON THE SUPERIOR ADVANTAGES DERIVED

FROM THE USE OF

IRON INSTEAD OF BRASS ORDNANCE

IN SUCH OPERATIONS.

BY
BREVET LT. COL. SIR JOHN MAY, K.C.B.
ROYAL HORSE ARTILLERY.

The Naval & Military Press Ltd

published in association with

FIREPOWER
The Royal Artillery Museum
Woolwich

Published by
The Naval & Military Press Ltd
Unit 10 Ridgewood Industrial Park,
Uckfield, East Sussex,
TN22 5QE England
Tel: +44 (0) 1825 749494
Fax: +44 (0) 1825 765701
www.naval-military-press.com

in association with

FIREPOWER
The Royal Artillery Museum, Woolwich
www.firepower.org.uk

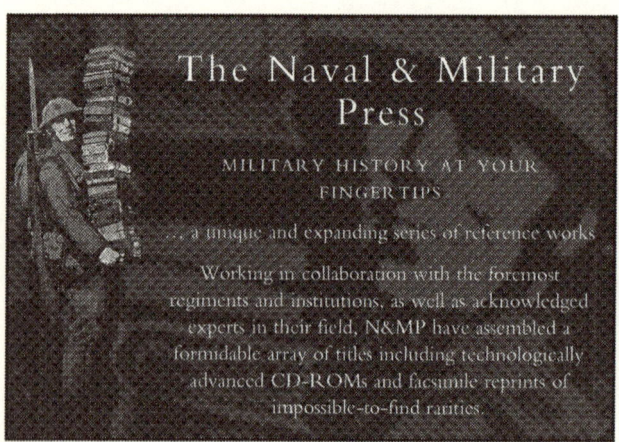

In reprinting in facsimile from the original, any imperfections are inevitably reproduced and the quality may fall short of modern type and cartographic standards.

A FEW

OBSERVATIONS

ON THE

MODE OF ATTACK,

AND EMPLOYMENT OF THE

HEAVY ARTILLERY

AT

CIUDAD RODRIGO AND BADAJOZ, IN 1812,
AND ST. SEBASTIAN, IN 1813;

WITH

A DISCUSSION ON THE SUPERIOR ADVANTAGES DERIVED

FROM THE USE OF

IRON INSTEAD OF BRASS ORDNANCE

IN SUCH OPERATIONS.

BY
BREVET LT. COL. SIR JOHN MAY, K.C.B.
ROYAL HORSE ARTILLERY.

LONDON:

PRINTED FOR T. EGERTON, BOOKSELLER TO THE ORDNANCE,
MILITARY LIBRARY, WHITEHALL.

1819.

CONTENTS.

INTRODUCTION . . . . *Page* 1

CHAPTER I.

On the Mode in which Ciudad Rodrigo and Badajoz were besieged in 1812, and St. Sebastian in 1813, and the manner of forming Breaches with Heavy Artillery, from a distance of between five and seven hundred yards 15

CHAPTER II.

On the greater Rapidity in reducing Places by this species of Siege, and a Discussion on the peculiar Properties of Brass and Iron Cannon 28

CHAPTER III.

Fortified Places to which such an Artillery or Accelerated Siege applies; Plan of the Attack, and Ordnance and Ammunition necessary for the Operation 35

CONTENTS.

Conclusion 43

References to Plan of Attack . . . . . 50—52

Plate I. Plan of the Attack for an Artillery Siege; and Estimate of Ordnance and Ammunition . 53

Plate II. Appearance which the *bottoms* of the Vents, or surface of the Metal, exhibited, in the examination of 3 iron 24-pounder guns, after firing 400 rounds each at Woolwich.

Plate III. Enlargement of the *tops* of the Vents of 21 iron 24-pounders, 2 iron 68-lb. carronades, and 4 brass 8-inch howitzers, English ordnance, employed against St. Sebastian.

Notes . . . . 57—74

INTRODUCTION.

THE peculiar mode of attack adopted by His Grace the Duke of Wellington in the sieges of Ciudad Rodrigo and Badajoz in 1812, causing them to fall much more rapidly than by a regular siege, completely baffled in both cases the calculations of the French Marshals opposed to him, who, though commanding superior armies, could not concentrate them and arrive in sufficient time to attempt the relief of these important fortresses.

The previous failure before Badajoz in 1811, under Lord Beresford, cannot be attributed to the plan of the attack, which was in itself essentially good, but to the insufficiency* and bad quality of the means employed in ordnance and ammunition to

* See Note (D), page 58.

reduce it, and particularly to the use of brass* instead of iron cannon.

The sieges therefore of Ciudad Rodrigo and Badajoz, the next year (1812), being undertaken with English iron ordnance, not only were the breaches made with a rapidity in vain attempted the preceding one, when the cylinders of the *brass* guns lost their shape, and consequently their accuracy in striking the object; but the bores remaining perfect in the *iron*, it will be seen in the following pages, that the advantage gained in such operations by the employ of English iron ordnance is *at least* four fold as to the quantity of ammunition that can be used from these *large calibres*, with the full charge, in a given time; and even more, if the tenacity of the metals be taken into the calculation, or what the brass battering pieces used at the time of Vauban, and those of England, France and other powers at this day, are capable of achieving.

By a French work published in 1817, the iron cannon of that nation seems to be

* This was Portuguese ordnance brought from the fortress of Elvas.

inferior to those used in the British service; and though employed in their navy has (strange to tell) never been contemplated as essential in sieges, notwithstanding brass ordnance of the larger calibres was proved by experiment in 1786, and since on service, to be incapable of the tenacity necessary to such operations.

If the above points be admitted, and the English battering ordnance be still improved by applying more durable vents, and removeable at pleasure,* few people will doubt that a much more rapid reduction of fortresses must follow, either by the regular or other attack, than has been hitherto calculated upon by military writers on the subject.

Did England possess great numbers of fortified places, and in cases of war were her troops more employed in their defence than in the attack of the enemy's, it would evidently be impolitic to show a power

* See the translation of Antoni on Artillery, chap. viii. page 153, wherein he treats especially on the vents of guns; and also page 71 of this work.

that may become an adversary the means by which such places could be more easily reduced; but as it is infinitely more in the attack than the defence of places that the British army is employed, a free discussion on such subjects may have its utility.

The writer is aware there is nothing novel in breaching a work from a distance, since it was the mode resorted to before the regular attack was practised and understood; and provided the breach were not defended, which was often the case, it mattered little, except in loss of time and ammunition, whether it was one or twenty days in forming,* so that the town capitulated upon the breach becoming practicable. It is however apparent, since the decrees issued by Louis XIV., the Republic and Buonaparte,† obliging the governors of places to stand at least one assault, consequently to retrench in every way the

* See the remarks on Marshal Berwick's sieges, in conclusion of the work.
† See Carnot's work "Sur la Defense des Places Fortes," 3d Edition, pages 5. 85. 89.

breach, which caused the principal difficulty in carrying recently the fortresses in Spain, that some rapid mode in the formation of the breach should be adopted by the besiegers; this obvious necessity therefore gave birth to the principles here laid down.

The British method commonly has been to reduce places by the system of battering in breach from a distance; but where this could not be effected on account of the regularity of the works, to oblige the town to capitulate by a heavy bombardment.

Seldom with the first mode have the necessary ricochet-batteries been sufficiently employed,* and therefore the enemy's artillery not altogether dismounted; the consequence has been in the assault that a greater loss of life was experienced than would have occurred under similar circumstances at a regular siege.

The observations contained in this work

* In Spain for want of transport to bring up the necessary means.

will distinctly show that they have no reference to a regular siege, but only to a species of attack which applies to *defects* that may be found in perhaps two-thirds of the fortresses in Europe and elsewhere, either in whole or in part of their works, which are said to be fortified in the *ancient way*, in distinction to what is called the modern improved manner, and which requires especially a regular siege to reduce.

In the latter operation the cannon is only an accessary, but in the former a principal agent.

Upon this basis therefore rests the system of attack here attempted to be detailed, wherein the rapidity of the siege will be shown greatly to keep pace with the powers of the iron cannon and the quantity of ammunition, in ricochet and from the breaching-battery, that can be fired from it in a much shorter time than could be attempted from the brass.

The number of mortars and howitzers estimated for this siege are given at one-fifth the whole of the ordnance; since, if they were double that proportion, and principally bombarded the town, which had a good garrison, though they might destroy great numbers of the inhabitants, yet they ought not to advance the taking of the place a single day: a better system would appear to be throughout the siege only to use them against the troops, to prevent the retrenchment of the bastion or the breach, and every part occupied by them looking towards it, thus leaving perfectly untouched the town.

With therefore the proper enfilades; the part to be breached not known by the enemy, and the breach formed rapidly in one day; a heavy ricochet and vertical fire to prevent its retrenchment; a LOW counterscarp and dry ditch; and the column of troops brought by approaches under cover close to it; there would appear little reason to infer that the loss of life by storming a breach made in this mode of attack would be materially greater than in the regular one. But should a parallel of casualties be drawn between the whole periods of such sieges, it would undoubtedly be in favour of the accelerated attack, since the duration of the regular siege would be to the other on a reduced calculation at least as five to one.

In the course of the work it will be found that French military writers have been particularly quoted; this has been done because the principal books on fortification and artillery, read in England and on the continent, are in that language; it therefore becomes interesting to inquire why they should be blindly and implicitly followed, since it is evident that the British, without suspecting it, by striking out methods of their own, have arrived at ameliorations in their service, and indeed in most of the mechanical arts, superior to their ingenious and warlike neighbours.

Though iron cannon has been used in the British navy, and for garrison service, at least a century past, yet the highly perfected state of the English iron ordnance, on an enlarged scale, does not bear date much farther back than the year 1797, when, from the previous establishment of the Inspector of Artillery's department, and his firmness in resisting the admission of this ordnance into the service without very severe proofs, many founders are stated to have been ruined by most of their guns bursting, thereby driving out of that employment such as had taken up their contracts without having the necessary knowledge to fulfil them. It is said that the Carron Company, previous to this period (in consequence of their guns bursting during the American war) were excluded by an Order in Council from furnishing guns to government; they however supplied the carronades, (fired with small charges,) which were of their invention, and in the mean time they furnished the East India Company; when, upon *these* guns being proved at Woolwich, it was noticed by the Inspector of Artillery, that they stood the proofs better than the ordnance of other founders, and were finished in every respect in a superior manner; which circumstance being represented to the Board of Ordnance by him, they were again admitted to a share in the government contracts, and they have continued principally, with Messrs. Walker and Co. these supplies ever since. The heavy iron ordnance is now paid for at the rate of from 18 to 20$l.$ per ton, and as the average price of brass ordnance is about 180$l.$ per ton for pieces above 10 cwt., the expense of the latter to the former is at least as nine to one—an economy of infinite importance to any state, but more particularly to one with so extensive a navy and such numerous colonies as Great Britain.

The next idea that naturally presents itself is, why, if the heavy iron ordnance be so much superior to, and cheaper than the brass, should not iron cannon be also adopted for the field service, and substituted for the lighter brass pieces, since there can be no doubt, if they resist the necessary proofs, they will be found superior in every respect to the brass, in their durability and unchangeable form in use of their bore. To understand this question there is one point to be taken into consideration which does not occur as to the heavy iron ordnance: it is, that as iron field-pieces would not have the same proportionate thickness of metal as the heavy iron guns, there would exist a necessity for these light iron ones being of such superior tenacity as to stand the most severe proofs.

It appears the Carron Company do not entertain the smallest doubt but that they could cast *iron field-pieces* of precisely the same weight* as the brass ones now in use, which iron guns they would warrant to stand whatever proofs might be considered necessary: but as the workmanship on the smaller calibres is proportionately more than that employed on the larger ones, and as in consequence of the superior refinement of the metal required in this case a greater loss of it in the furnace would take place; therefore 56*l*.† per ton, being at the

* A cubic foot of gun-metal weighs 549 lbs.; that of cast-iron 464 lbs.

† No doubt by a proper competition between the founders this price might be much diminished.

rate of 6*d*. a lb., is the price at which the company would cast these guns: now as the *brass* field pieces cost about 200*l*. a ton, the proportionate expense of one to the other would be nearly as one to four, or, in other words, *iron* field-pieces may be cast for about one-fourth the expense of what the brass ones now cost.

In considering this question, however, it is necessary to state, though the heavy brass guns will, by the French experiments given in La Martillière's book,* be found to be nearly useless for the purpose of sieges; yet this is by no means the case as to brass pieces for field service, which are much more durable on account of the smaller quantities of powder fired from them, and the inferior weight of their shot, these pieces being equal to several actions: it is nevertheless observed that their cylinders are scored considerably by the use of cannister shot; and that when spherical case shot burst in them they are oftentimes

---

* See Note (H), page 61.

rendered unserviceable, and also that they are gradually more or less damaged in proportion to their being fired, until, for these reasons, they become useless by the enlargements of their bores; whereas it may be fairly inferred, from the few defects found upon the examination of the *iron* 24-pounders used at St. Sebastian, that *iron field*-pieces, as to their bore, would remain unchanged even after 2 or 3000 rounds; consequently, in every stage of their use, they would be found to be infinitely better pieces of ordnance than the brass ones.

The price paid by government for carronades is at the rate of 26*l.* per ton; the extra expense above that demanded for heavy ordnance being on account of workmanship.

Some few trials have been made at Woolwich with guns of wrought-iron, but they have not succeeded, from the difficulty of welding and hammering in a uniform manner so large a body while heated; besides, the greater price of such ordnance, even if well made, would be a bar to its adoption. (G.)

It was not originally the writer's intention to have said so much generally on the different calibres of brass and iron ordnance, but only of those employed in sieges; the fact however is, that in such a discussion an inquiry into the qualities of the one becomes so connected with those of the other, that to separate them would be to leave the matter very inconclusive and imperfect.

CHAPTER I.

On the Mode in which Ciudad Rodrigo and Badajoz were besieged in 1812 and St. Sebastian in 1813, and the Manner of forming Breaches with Heavy Artillery from a Distance of between five and seven hundred yards.

To take a town fortified in a *regular* manner according to the modern system, that is to say, a place that has the scarp walls well hid by the counterscarp and glacis, the only certain and efficacious mode is by the different parallels and sap, the ricochet and vertical fire, and afterwards from the crest of the glacis to batter in breach.

*But this method seems by no means necessary against such places as Ciudad Rodrigo, Badajoz or St. Sebastian, which are fortified in

---

* See Lieutenant Colonel Jones's Journals of the Sieges undertaken by the Allies in Spain in the years 1811, 1812, and 1813. These remarks as to Badajoz only apply to the last siege of that fortress in 1812.

the old way, and where from five to seven hundred yards some portions of the scarp of the walls were seen uncovered to their foot, or nearly so, and consequently could be battered in breach from that distance; otherwise, if it be requisite to take the same slow means to reduce badly fortified places as good ones, wherein lies the advantage of the modern improvements? besides the superior height of the walls above the glacis, renders the ricochet-batteries less efficacious, and therefore the mode in which such a place is fortified should, according to this reasoning, be more capable of resisting a *regular* attack, than if constructed in the modern improved manner.

The principal improvement in fortification evidently took its rise from the necessity of covering the walls of a town against being breached from a distance, thereby reducing the enemy to lose much time before he is enabled to bring his heavy artillery on the crest of the glacis to effect by a breach a passage into the place.

It results then, from this view of the subject, that the one is an engineer, and the other more an artillery operation.*

* In calling this mode of attack more an *artillery* operation,

The attack of a place fortified in the old way with dry ditches, appears to be more an artillery than an engineer operation, because there exists no necessity for the second and third parallel, &c., but it is particularly so from the advantages to be gained in time by the employment of a powerful train of artillery, not only to extinguish the enemy's fire, but to make a breach rapidly in *one* or at the *utmost two days*, and assault the evening it is practicable, preventing thereby the retrenchment of the same.

The flank-breach formed at Ciudad Rodrigo in a day and a half, (and if more artillery had been used it might have been effected in *one* day) and the curtain-breach at Badajoz in one day, are examples of the advantages gained by such rapidity, since to neither does the enemy appear to have had time to create the usual obstacles; but if a breach, from the strength of the wall, require *two* days to render it practicable, a most heavy fire from mortars and howitzers should be kept

it is necessary not to be misunderstood,—it relates to the *material*, and not the *personal*, and may be characterized by this name on account of the great mass of ordnance or guns proposed to be brought forward to act on one point, and the effects the fire of such artillery should produce in the quick formation of a breach towards the *rapid* reduction of the place.

upon it all the intervening night and following day.

It would appear that one large and well-formed breach is perfectly sufficient, particularly when made in a day,—and as the enemy's ordnance will be dismounted if the requisite artillery in ricochet be employed, there is no other material obstacle to entering the town than the descent into the ditch,* and the resistance from behind the open breach.

The mode in which the three places in question were besieged has been said with truth to have caused greater casualties than if more time had been given, and the attack been *regular*,—but most of this loss must be attributed to the means in artillery being in no case sufficient,† except at the *second* part of the siege of St. Sebastian. Had mortars and howitzers, with

---

* Generally speaking, few fortifications where the scarp is completely seen from a distance, have a counterscarp of much height; besides in the rear of each place of arms and salient angle of the covered-way there are steps of communication into the ditch, which, unless cut away at the beginning of the siege to facilitate sorties, which is not practised, it might be nearly impossible to do so, during the operation of breaching, and if left till night it would be too late, as the assault would then be given.—*See on this subject* note (K). page 71.

† Want of transport was the principal reason why more artillery was not brought forward at the sieges.

more cannon, been employed at Ciudad Rodrigo—an increase of battering-ordnance and a large proportion of mortars at Badajoz—and the quantity of artillery at the last attack of St. Sebastian been there at the first, all these places might have been carried, no doubt, with as little loss of life, and we know, in much less time, than by a regular siege, so absolutely necessary against a modern fortified place, but not against the more ancient ones.

The reason why mortars were not allowed to be made use of at Ciudad Rodrigo and Badajoz, was from a motive of humanity, these towns being inhabited by the Spaniards, our allies.

But though a proportion of mortars and howitzers should in all cases form a constituent part of a battering train, yet when a place be sufficiently garrisoned, it is not against the town but only for the destruction of the enemy's artillery, to prevent a breach being retrenched, and to clear all impediments as to fire in going to the assault, that their powerful effects should be employed.

The fire from 59 pieces of heavy ordnance, 20 of which were 10-inch mortars, in two hours caused the surrender of the castle of St. Sebastian, which, from its scarped height and great difficulty of situation, would probably have resisted some days, had not this vertical fire been brought against it.

That a large breach may be formed in *one*, or at the utmost *two* days, from between five and seven hundred yards, with a given number of guns, is easy to be shown by the practice of the above sieges.*

Time of firing at Ciudad Rodrigo.

On the 16th Jan. 1812, at this place the sun rose at 16 minutes past 8 o'clock, and set at 54 minutes past 4, giving 8 hours and 38 minutes for the time of firing, or for calculation 8 hours and a half.

	Hours.
Jan. 14, 1812. Firing from 20 24-prs. and 2 18-prs.	1
15. The whole day, from 23 24-prs. and 2 18-prs. to form the great breach	$8\frac{1}{2}$
16. Foggy weather, firing from 23 24-prs. and 2 18-prs.	1
17. Foggy weather, firing from 23 24-prs. and 2 18-prs. but cleared up at noon	5
18. Clear weather, from 30 24-prs. and 2 18-prs. to form large and small breach	$8\frac{1}{2}$
19. Clear weather, from 30 24-prs.—at 4 P.M. both breaches considered as practicable, fire turned on defences, and place assaulted at 7 P.M.	$8\frac{1}{2}$
Total firing hours	$32\frac{1}{2}$

* A return of the Ordnance employed and Expenditure of Ammunition at these sieges will be found in Table III. page 54.

There was expended at this siege 8,950 24-pounder and 565 18-pounder round shot, making a total of 9,515 rounds.

At the siege of St. Sebastian, in the month of July, 1813, there was about $15\frac{1}{2}$ hours daylight, where from 300 to 350* rounds were constantly fired from an iron 24-pounder gun in battering; and therefore, allowing the smaller proportion of 300 rounds expenditure in $15\frac{1}{2}$ hours, 164 rounds would be fired in $8\frac{1}{2}$ hours or during daylight.

By the total of rounds expended at Ciudad Rodrigo, it appears that 292·76 rounds were fired from the ordnance in each of the $32\frac{1}{2}$ hours in battering or otherwise.

Three hours firing, or 878 rounds, being given for the defences, and one-fourth of the remain-

* There is no reason why many more rounds could not be fired from these guns in the same space of time, since by so doing (as will be shown hereafter) the cylinders would not have been damaged, nor would the guns have acquired such a degree of heat as to fire the powder in the cartridge:— a wet sponge however should be constantly used in loading, and *tubes* to fire the charge instead of priming powder, which assists materially in damaging the vents.—In the experiments made at Woolwich to ascertain the best vent for iron guns, 50 rounds were fired in 147 minutes, which is at the rate of 489 rounds in 24 hours.—*See* Table of PROOF TRIAL, page 54.

ing time and ammunition viz. 2,159 rounds for the flank or small breach (that breach being 30 feet wide and the large one 100), there will then remain 6,478 rounds for the great breach.

Thus 40 24-pounders, iron, with an expenditure of 164 rounds to each, being 6,560, would have more than rendered the large breach practicable in $8\frac{1}{4}$ hours or during daylight.

But supposing 878 rounds to be more than was fired at the defences, and even allowing this quantity together with 6,560 rounds to have been expended upon the great breach, i. e. a total of 7,438 rounds, then 46 24-pounders would undoubtedly have rendered it practicable in $8\frac{1}{2}$ hours.

The two breaches were formed from a distance of between five hundred and five hundred and sixty yards.

Time of firing at Badajoz.

On the 4th April, 1812, the sun rose at 7 minutes past 6, and set at 6 minutes past 7, being from rising to setting 12 hours 59 minutes, or for calculation 13 hours for battering.

				Hours.
Mar. 30.	No. 9. ——	8 18-pounders	. .	13
31.	—— ——	8 18-prs. ⎫		
	No. 7. ——	12 24-prs. ⎬ 26 guns	.	13
	No. 8. ——	6 18-prs. ⎭		
Apr. 1.	—— ——	—— 26 guns as before		13
2.	—— ——	—— do.	. .	13
3.	—— ——	—— do.	. .	13
4.	—— ——	—— do.	. .	13
5.	—— ——	—— do.	. .	13
6.	—— ——	—— do. 14 of ⎫ which to form curtain breach . ⎭		13
			Total	104

There was expended, of round shot, at this siege 18,832 24-pounders and 13,029 18-pounders, making a total of 31,861 rounds.

The three breaches (of which the curtain one was 40 feet wide, the flank 90 feet, and the large one in the face of a bastion 150 feet) were rendered practicable from a distance of between 6 and 700 yards.

Fourteen of the iron 18-pounders used for

battering were Russian guns, (but mounted on English travelling carriages), and cast at Carron in Scotland; the shot fired from them were principally English; and as the calibre and consequent windage (A) were greater with the English shot, they did not strike the wall with so much force as if projected from British ordnance of the same nature.

It is also necessary to remark on the superior effects of the 24-pounder shot over the 18-pounders, with proportionate charges from Russian or English guns, since 13,029 rounds of the latter ammunition was expended in battering; but notwithstanding the disadvantage of an increased windage and so much 18-pounder instead of all 24-pounder shot being used, it will be seen that a certain number of 24-pounders iron guns, would have made the large breach in 13 hours; it is, consequently, not necessary to enter into any calculation of the relative effects of the two ammunitions on a wall, more than to show that these points have not been overlooked in the discussion.

As 6 24-pounders and 4 18-pounders, besides some of the 16 24-pounder iron howitzers, were used in enfilade, about $\frac{1}{4}$* of the 31,861 24 and

* It is, perhaps rather overrated at one fourth, but this proportion is given on account of so much 18-pounder round shot forming part of the 31,861 rounds.

18-pounder shot may be said to have been expended in that manner, thus leaving 23,896 rounds to form the three breaches.

It has been shown that the curtain breach of 40 feet was made on the 6th of April by 14 guns, and a consequent expenditure of 3,514 rounds; there then remains 20,382 rounds for the other two breaches.

The flank-breach* was 90 feet, and the large one 150 feet, therefore, as the former was in the proportion of 3 to 5 of the latter, it surely will be allowed that time and ammunition was expended upon it; there then remains 12,230 rounds for the great breach.

Suppose then 50 iron 24-pounders to have been put in battery to breach with the proportionate expenditure of 251 rounds in 13 hours, being 12,550 rounds, the large breach of 150 feet would have been more than complete in 13 hours by 320 rounds.

It is evident, therefore, even in this case, and with so large a breach† that a second day's bat-

* The flank-breach, though smaller, was, in proportion to its size, more difficult to form than the large one, on account of the piers of some casemates it was necessary to breach through.

† A breach of 150 feet is much larger than will be genenerally required; one sufficiently wide for the front of a co-

tering and consequent expenditure of 25,100 rounds from the 50 24-pounders could not be necessary.

Time of Firing at the First part of the Siege of St. Sebastian, in July 1813.

On the 21st July, the Sun rose at 31 minutes past 4, and set at 2 minutes past 8, being, from rising to setting, 15 hours and 31 minutes, or for calculation 15 hours and a half.

	Hours.
July 20th, battering the whole day from 20 24-prs.	15½
21, ———— do. ———— do.	15½
22, ———— do. ———— do. The large breach of 100 feet practicable this evening	15½
23, The 20 guns turned to form small breach of 30 feet, also practicable this evening	15½
Time of firing.	62

The time of firing and number of guns made use of fully explain themselves, for we see 20

lumn of about 30 men to move up abreast appears a good sized one, which, by allowing a distance of 3 feet for each man, would give a breadth of 90 feet; it must, however, be taken into consideration, that a breach rendered practicable from a distance of between 6 and 700 yards cannot be cut so accurately as one formed from the crest of a glacis, consequently the size in the former case should be larger than in the latter.

24-pounders (six of which were ship-guns from the Surveillante Frigate) employed firing for 4 days, about half a day was at the defences of the town and a whole one (as seen above) in forming the small breach, leaving thereby, $2\frac{1}{2}$ days for the large one, which, at 20 guns a day, gives 50 guns.

Therefore supposing that number of iron 24-pounders to have been put in battery together, the 50 would evidently have rendered the great breach of 100 feet practicable in one day, which 20 guns were proportionately $2\frac{1}{2}$ days in achieving.—(B.)

It perhaps may be well here to remark that the six ship-guns were fired with a charge of 6lbs. instead of 8lbs. the quantity for the other 24-pounders, these ship-guns being lighter and shorter than those with the train, consequently their effects with the smaller charge from a distance were not so great as with the larger one.—(C.)

The breaches were made from a distance of about 600 yards.

CHAPTER II.

On the greater Rapidity in reducing places by this species of Siege, and a Discussion on the peculiar Properties of Brass and Iron Cannon.

UPON a reference to the three sieges in question it will be seen that in allowing the principle of a sufficiency of artillery for the breaching-battery (say 50 iron 24-pounders), forming only one large breach, and doing so in a day; that Ciudad Rodrigo could in that case have been assaulted on the evening of the 15th Jan. 1812, being seven days from the breaking ground before it; whereas, by the time occupied in making the two breaches with smaller means, it was not taken until 4 days afterwards.

At Badajoz the breaches were began on the 30th March, 1812, the place might, therefore, by the above principles, have been assaulted the same evening, making 13 days from the beginning of the siege, whereas, from the small means in artillery, the breaches were not completed until 7 days afterwards.

At the first part of the siege of St. Sebastian, ground was broken before it on the night between the 13th and 14th July 1813, the first breach was commenced on the 20th, and had there been a sufficiency of artillery the place could have been assaulted the same evening, the 7th day, whereas the two breaches were not practicable until three days afterwards.

Circumstances caused the Duke of Wellington to adopt this mode of attack instead of the *regular* one, for had he not resorted to it, it is evident from the history of the campaigns, he must have fought battles for Ciudad Rodrigo and Badajoz, or been under the necessity of raising those sieges, which battles would have cost him infinitely more men than he would have lost before both places with less efficient means than he had: it is, however, of the very first importance to a General to gain time in such an operation as a siege, particularly when, by anticipating his enemy, he becomes thereby master of the place; it consequently is a matter of much interest to inquire the difference of time taken by his Grace and the French in reducing two of the same fortresses, they having done so by the *regular mode of attack*.

On the 11th June 1810, Marshal Massena broke ground before Ciudad Rodrigo, and the place *capitulated* after a breach was made on the 10th July, but *not assaulted*, thus holding out 29 days.

Marshal Mortier commenced the siege of Badajoz on the 28th January 1811, and it surrendered on the 10th of March, upon a breach of 25 feet wide being made in a curtain, *without having been assaulted*, on the 41st day.

The Duke of Wellington by an *irregular* mode of attack, took the former place by *assault* (after two breaches were formed) in 11 days, being 18 days less than the French.

In the same manner Badajoz was taken *by storm* (after 3 breaches were made in its walls) in 20 days, being 21 less than the French.

Thus the duke became master of both these places in less than half the time the French were about them.

It was at the *first* part of the siege of St. Sebastian these ideas struck the writer forcibly, and he communicated them to a friend in England. Where the small proportion of ordnance that could be brought forward was inadequate to the result expected; they had, however, gained some strength from previous observations at Ciudad Rodrigo and Badajoz in 1812, of the superior efficacy of our much improved English *iron* guns for battering.—Monsieur de Bousmard*, one of the latest and best of the French authors on fortification says, 'that in battering from *brass* 24-pounders only from 100 to 120 rounds per gun can be fired in 24 hours;' but, as before quoted, it will be seen that from 300 to 350 rounds were fired from *iron* 24-pounders in 15 hours and a half from a distance of between 5 and 700 yards; this, it is true, in 8 days battering at Badajoz and 9 days at St. Sebastian, so increased the size of the vents that two or three fingers might have been inserted in them, but in every other respect the guns were perfectly serviceable, (E) and in their bore kept their form, so much so that in this state at the last siege of St. Sebastian their great accuracy in firing over the heads of the troops with safety as they stood on the breach, at the French who were behind a retrenchment at a little distance from and a few feet above them, was particularly mentioned by Lord Lynedock in his dispatch.

To facilitate this inquiry it may, perhaps, be proper to go back to the time of Vauban, who is followed as having practised and taught the best *regular* mode of attacking a place, and to

---

* See his edition of the Memorial de Cormontaigne, dated 1 May, 1801, note, page 37.

quote a cotemporary writer on artillery, Monsieur de S. Remi, who says, in speaking of brass ordnance for battering, " Les pieces de 24 font un très bon effet, lorsqu'on ne les éloigne que de 100 toises de l'ouvrage qu'elles battent en brêche; mais audelà de la portée de 150 toises (300 yards) on n'y parviendroit plus, les coups n'ayant plus assez de force pour cela."

And again, " Je suppose que l'on batte en brêche une face de bastion avec 10 ou 12 pieces de 24, dont on tire de chacune par jour 90 à 100 coups, il faudra quelquefois plus de 12 à 15 jours avant que cette brêche soit praticable."

Thus requiring from 10 to 18,000 rounds of 24-pounder ammunition at the short distance of from 2 to 300 yards, and from 12 to 15 days to render a breach practicable.

If, therefore, in Vauban's and St. Remi's time not more than from 90 to 100 rounds a gun from brass ordnance could be fired in 24 hours, and the velocity given to the shot would have little effect beyond 300 yards, it is evident that both the powder (F) and ordnance must be much inferior to the *iron* guns (G) and powder used at the forementioned sieges, since we see there at *least four* times the quantity of ammunition employed without material injury to the piece, and that at an object of more than double the distance.

Brass ordnance does not appear to have been ameliorated since the period quoted; but iron ordnance, then not made use of in a siege and not to be relied upon, has now certainly been brought to great perfection, and promises even to be more so; yet these durable qualities in cast iron, though so peculiarly adapted to sieges, have been almost entirely overlooked by every military writer.

The battering-train employed by the French against Ciudad Rodrigo in June 1810, and taken afterwards in that fortress, was of brass. (H.)

The arts have given smoother surfaces and more mathematical precision to the forms of ordnance, the bore, shot, and shells: if, therefore, the foregoing premises be admitted, it follows, that while fortresses, in their construction and strength, are nearly the same as at the time of Vauban, the *battering artillery* has been improved *four-fold* and the powder fully double, and that their consequent influence on the attack of places towards their more rapid reduction, in the *regular* or *other* manner, becomes apparent. For if it be proved,—That the cylinders of iron guns support the most severe firing without altering their form—

That from 4 to 500 rounds in the 24 hours with the large charge can be fired from an iron 24-pounder, while, at the same time, not more than from 100 to 120 rounds can from the brass, and even with that number the bore is injured—

That in one kind of siege the cannon is shown to be a principal agent towards the reduction of the place, whereas in a regular one it is only an accessary—

It surely should follow that the comparative rapidity of the reduction of places by the *Accelerated* or *Artillery* mode of attack will keep pace with the powers of the iron cannon over the brass: and though not in the same degree at a *regular siege*, yet as the iron ordnance is a better tool or engine to work with, its effects surer, and what is to be achieved can be done in a shorter space of time, the regular siege ought also to be quickened and abridged by such means, or in other words, the calculations as to time entered into by the French and other military writers on sieges, wherein only the brass ordnance are supposed to be used, no longer appear to hold good. (I.)

The costliness of brass ordnance was the reason of the substitution of iron in its place in England, and the proofs which the latter undergoes to ascertain its strength and tenacity, have brought it to its present point of perfection.

CHAPTER III.

Fortified Places to which such an Artillery or Accelerated Siege applies; Plan of the Attack, and Ordnance and Ammunition necessary for the operation.

IT now remains to be shown in what manner a place should be besieged by what has been termed an irregular attack, but which may more aptly be described as an artillery or accelerated one, in distinction to that of a *regular* siege;

What is the necessary proportion of ordnance and ammunition ;—

And to what description of fortresses does such an artillery or accelerated attack apply.

This kind of attack would appear fully to apply to great numbers of fortresses on the continent of Europe, built before the modern improvements in fortification, situated on a height or level ground, whose walls being uncovered to their foot or nearly so, can be battered in breach from a distance—

To fortresses, where, though good in most parts, there may be, from some oversight or other reason, the abovementioned defects—

Where, to pass to the assault of the breach,

there is not a complication of outworks of a regular construction, but only a simple front with bastion, ra elin and covert-way; should, however, the scarp of the outworks be completely seen, they may be breached successively, or if the means be sufficient at the same time, from a distance.

Where the counterscarp before or near a breach is not more than from 10 to 12 feet high and the ditch a dry one (K.)—

Where there is space before the front attacked to place the breaching-batteries of 50 *iron* 24-pounders in one line, in echelon, or on different heights, so that in case there be a necessity for a battery being at 800 yards, the nearest of a similar size may be at 400, thus making an average distance of 600 yards.

Should it so happen that the ground be unfavourable for the ricochet-batteries, these guns, &c. may be brought together in a good situation, so as by a powerful concentrated *direct* fire to destroy the enemy's artillery and indeed the work covering it, in which, if necessary, the breaching-battery of 50 guns (L) might take a part before it be opened on the wall to be breached.

This artillery or accelerated attack also applies particularly to where old fortresses or forts are placed in the enemy's colonies, and perhaps to many constructed by the natives of India: it is peculiarly adapted to a maritime people, since if the place be near the sea and necessity requires it, the extra-battering ordnance and men to work it can be obtained from large ships of war, as was done in a small way at St. Sebastian, and as was the case in Lord Peterborough's reduction of Barcelona, to the number of 51 pieces of cannon.*

The proportion† of ordnance and ammunition for such an attack will, as the front embraced be not so great, nor the duration of the siege so long, be less in ordnance than for a *regular* one, but infinitely so as to the quantity of ammunition,‡ even though 4 days for ricochet and 2 days for battering were required, whereas

---

* See Captain Carleton's Memoirs, page 147.

† See the estimate for ordnance and ammunition, page 53.

‡ See " Mémorial pour l'Attaque des Places, ouvrage postume de Cormontaigne," 1815. And the " Tableau d'Approvisionnemens de siège, A & B," at the end of the volume. Vauban's estimate for a siege of a month was 168 pieces: there is also shown what were brought to besiege five large places, with the ordnance and ammunition expended. The proportion of ordnance sent from England for the regular siege of Dantzic in 1813, and made use of by the allies, was 214 pieces, of which 100 were iron 24-pounders, 20 12-pounders, 28 howitzers, and 66 mortars.

it may be inferred, from former observations, that 3 days from the ricochet-batteries and 1 from the breaching-battery, would be sufficient.

In this mode of attack there appears only a necessity for a first parallel at about 600 yards from the salient angle of the bastion, in which parallel, the ricochet and mortar batteries will be placed, and a boyau run in advance clear of the fire from the breaching-battery, so as to carry as far forward as possible the troops going to the assault. It will be seen by a reference to the plan of attack (see Plate I.) that some of the ordnance for ricochet would, if not otherwise disposed of, fire over the breaching battery from the first parallel, and it therefore will be necessary to place these pieces at once on the site where that battery will afterwards be established.

The time of the operation is given largely at 6 days, but 5 days would be ample, provided there be only 1 day employed in breaching, which, except in a most extraordinary case, would be sufficient. On account of some formidable outworks where this mode of attack does not apply (even though the wall be seen to the foot) but the engineers are obliged to reduce them in a *regular* manner, these works once in their possession, and the rampart of the place uncovered, they may perhaps save themselves much time and labour, and surprise the enemy by breaching from a distance, and running forward from the sap or work a gallery to the counterscarp and blow it in the moment the troops are going to the assault, thus giving the siege a double character.

From the foregoing Observations the following PRINCIPLES *appear to present themselves—*

1st. That a town simply fortified with bastions, ravelin and covert-way, having a low counterscarp and dry ditch, with the scarp of the walls seen to the foot or nearly so, should, to save time in besieging it, be battered in breach from a distance.

2d. That in this mode of attack the usual operations of the Engineer at a *regular* siege may be greatly abridged, since there is only a necessity for a first parallel, in which and near it may be placed the ricochet and breaching batteries, carrying forward rapidly (clear of your own fire) an approach, so as to place as much in advance as possible the column of troops for the assault of the breach. On the spot where the second parallel is usually drawn, some field-pieces might be placed, to assist in repelling sorties from the garrison.

3d. That the breaching-battery, at a distance of about 600 yards, should not be less* than 50 iron 24-pounders, increasing the proportion of ordnance for the siege with the requisite guns, mortars, and howitzers; since though we have seen that the curtain breach at Badajoz was effected by 14 guns in 13 hours, and the small one of 30 feet at St. Sebastian in $15\frac{1}{2}$ hours, from 20 guns, on that and on the defences; yet as by previous calculation it has been found that the large breach of 150 feet in the face of a bastion at the former place would have required 50 24-pounders to form the same in 13 hours, and a similar number of guns at St. Sebastian, that quantity of guns is assumed as necessary for the breaching-battery.

4th. That as it is most important the breaching-battery should not be opened until it be found that the ricochet ones have had the ef-

---

* It must be kept in view that the whole of this reasoning as to the attack, ordnance and ammunition, applies to a fortress of magnitude—since it is evident a much less number of guns would effect a breach in *one* day through a work whose walls are known to be badly built and not of the usual thickness.

fect of destroying the enemy's artillery looking to the part to be breached or the advance to it—this service well performed, there is every reason to infer that the loss of life incident to the storming a breach with this mode of attack would not be much greater than in the regular one, since the former breach will be made more rapidly, and the obstacles behind it consequently less, and if the shorter duration of the artillery attack be taken into computation, the whole amount of casualties would be less in this than in a regular siege.

5th. That every effort on the part of the commanding officer of artillery should be made to render a large breach practicable in *one* day, by not opening the breaching-battery until the whole of the 50 24-pounders be ready, with at least 300 rounds to each close at hand, to begin the fire at dawn of day, and not to finish until dark, and during this time to give one relief in men. (M.)

6th. That during the formation of the breach a large proportion of the mortars and howitzers should play upon the space immediately behind and upon the right and left of it, so as effectually to prevent the enemy from retrenching the same; and in case the wall, from its hardness and thickness, require a second day's battering, the whole of the vertical fire should be turned upon it during the intervening night and following day until the breach become practicable.

7th. In case, however, that the town to be besieged be not near the sea, or so situated that a large battering-train can be collected sufficient to form a great breach in *one*, or at the utmost *two* days, from a distance, and to dismount the enemy's artillery, the place, though badly fortified, should be besieged in as regular a manner as a good one, to save a great sacrifice in men, and perhaps, ultimately, the necessity of raising the siege.

8th. The result of these observations then is, either that an efficient battering-train must be employed, so as with certainty to effect the reduction of the place in, *at most, six days;* or that in consequence of the want of such means, the town must be besieged in a *regular* manner, thus leaving nothing to hazard, but increasing most materially the period of its holding out, thereby reducing the question to *time* or *means*.

CONCLUSION.

Since these observations were written, a remark was made by a friend to whom they were shown, that the sieges carried on by the Duke of Berwick against Nice, Barcelona, and St. Sebastian, were principally what are here termed the Artillery or Irregular kind, bearing a strong resemblance to the late ones in the Peninsula; upon turning to the Memoirs, we find—

That the siege of the citadel of Nice, in 1705, was in character an artillery or irregular one.

16th Nov. Ground was broken before it.
8th Dec. On account of the difficulty of the soil and few workmen, the batteries were not finished and opened until this date . . . . 22 days.
6th Jan. There were effected 3 large practicable breaches, when the governor, seeing dispositions making for the assault, capitulated; being 29 days firing on the defences and in forming the 3 breaches . . . 29 days.

The place was thus taken in 51 days without an assault.

The ordnance for the siege was 70 heavy guns and 16 mortars, making a total of 86 pieces of cannon, with an expenditure of 700,000 lbs. of powder.

Remark.—The distances at which the breaching-batteries were placed, were from 200 to 300 toises; the breaches (though so long in rendering practicable) were extremely large and good, as the Marshal says, " pour faire voir que je ne m' étais point trompé, je montais à cheval avec 50 officiers jusqu'au haut de la brèche."— The means in artillery at the above distances were sufficient for making the breaches, since the governor capitulated, but as they were from first to last 29 days in forming, had the besieged only employed a part of that time in mining and retrenching, and stood an assault, it seems doubtful whether the place would have been carried; therefore, trying this siege by the before-mentioned principles, this was a very hazardous mode of attack, since neither the Duke's cannon were in sufficient number or goodness, nor his powder of that quality to ensure, from the distances at which his batteries were placed, the rapid formation of a breach in *one* or at the utmost *two* days.

His army consisted of 16 very weak battalions, bad troops, the garrison was 2,000 men, and the loss on each side about 600 men.

---

*The siege of St. Sebastian, in 1719, was an artillery operation.

Night between the 19th and 20th
    July, ground broken before it.
25th July. The batteries opened . . 5 days.
  1st Aug. Breaches practicable, town
    surrendered, and garrison retired
    to the castle . . . . 7 days.
19th Aug. Castle forced to capitulate
    by bombardment . . . . . . 18 days.

The place thus was taken in 30 days without an assault.

---

* The relation of the sieges of Nice and Barcelona is by the Duke of Berwick himself, and well detailed; but that of St. Sebastian is imperfect, by another hand, and compiled after his death from his correspondence with the French ministers, &c.

There is no mention made of the quantity of ordnance employed, nor the number or size of the breaches.

The breaching-batteries were said to have been placed at the distance of 180 toises, about 360 yards.

Remark.—Since the breaches were 7 days in forming, it is evident, the governor might have retrenched them and stood an assault, in which case the same observations apply as at the siege of Nice.

The siege of Barcelona, in 1714, bears the double character of a regular, and artillery or irregular attack.

The Marshal says, " Je me determinai donc au côté de la marine, qui regarde le Besos, attendu que le front n'étoit que de 3 bastions, dont les courtines élevées donnoient beaucoup *de prise au canon,* et que le fossé n'avoit que 6 *pieds de profondeur.* Les approches en étoient beaucoup plus faciles, par rapport à *de petites buttes,* derrière lesquelles l'on pouvait mettre plusieurs bataillons à couvert."

Night between the 12th and 13th July,
   broke ground.
25th July. The batteries of 80 pieces
   of cannon opened on 3 bastions . 13 days.
30th July. A lodgment made on the
   covert-way.
12th Aug. A breach was practicable in
   the bastion of St. Claire, and a
   mine sprung under the flanked
   angle of Porte Neuve; the two
   bastions were assaulted and carried both on this day and the 13th,
   but the troops were driven out
   again before a lodgment could
   be completed . . . . 17 days.

   Total of regular attack 30 days.

The Duke here observes, " La vigoureuse ré-
sistance des ennemis me détermina à ne plus
hasarder de pareilles attaques; mais aussi il étoit
difficile de savoir comment on pourroit autre-
ment se rendre maître de la place ——— pour
toute ressource (on) me proposa de donner un as-
saut général à une brêche de 30 toises qu'il y
avoit à la courtine entre Porte Neuve et St.
Claire; on voyait bien que la tête devoit avoir
tourné à quiconque pouvait faire une pareille pro-
position, car les flancs étaient dans leur entier,

la brêche minée, et de plus il y avoit derrière un très bon retranchement autre deux coupures sur le rempart aux deux côtés de la brêche.—Enfin, après m'être bien promené et bien pensé, je me déterminai à ouvrir tellement le point de l'attaque que l'on peut, pour ainsi dire, y entrer en bataille. Ainsi, sans m'exposer à de nouveaux échecs, j'allais surement en besogne, *j'avançai donc quelques batteries* et m' armai de patience."

Artillery or Irregular Attack.

From the 13th Aug. to the 11th Sept. battering in breach, during which time *seven* large breaches were rendered practicable, and on the last day two out of the three bastions were carried by assault: the place was allowed upon this success to surrender at discretion . . . . 30 days.

Thus Barcelona held out against the two attacks 60 days.

The garrison of the town amounted to 16,000 men, in most part soldiers; the Duke of Berwick's army was large and his loss great.

Remark.—The length of time the breaches in the regular attack were making was the reason why the bastion and curtain breaches were so strongly retrenched, and the two assaults thereby rendered null, which, together with not having destroyed the fire on the flanks, it appears, obliged the Duke to open, by means of his artillery, such a portion of the rampart as to place his troops in the breaches in great force.

Since, however, he had 87 heavy guns, and began by the regular attack, consequently was very near the place, and seeing the foot of the rampart, had he put most of this artillery in battery at a *short* distance in the first instance, to form only *one* large breach, it would appear probable that with such means, and at such a distance, he might have been able to have effected a breach at the utmost in two days, thereby preventing its retrenchment.

It is very evident from these sieges, that neither the cannon nor the powder were equal to what were recently made use of in Spain, though the breaches made by the Duke of Berwick were of an extraordinary size as well as their number great.

These three places were near the sea, which gave every facility in assembling large battering-trains.

References to the Plan of Attack.

(See Plate I.)

It is obvious that were the angles of the bastions, ravelin and covered-ways more obtuse, many of the ricochet-batteries would not fall on the same spot with the breaching ones; but these angles are purposely shown so acute for the better understanding the foregoing observations.

It is conceived that a ricochet and vertical fire on the intermediate ravelin of 4 24-pounders, 2 8-inch howitzers and 5 10-inch mortars, viz. 11 heavy pieces, with a great expenditure of ammunition for 3 or 4 days, would render that work untenable, consequently facilitate the advance of the storming party; indeed during the assault, if conceived necessary, 10 or 12 24-pounders might be turned upon it from the breaching-batteries—

That as the fire from the breaching-batteries passes into and over the covered-ways opposite the face of the bastion to be breached and that of the ravelin looking towards it, these covered-ways could not be held by any troops while the breaching was in operation, nor would they have time to take post there during the very short cessation of fire, and the assailants rushing to the assault—

That the flank of the bastion enfilading the breach, though short, would in all probability have its ordnance dismounted and be breached, since it has on it from 2 to 4 24-pounders in ricochet and a direct fire of 4 of the like ordnance throughout the siege—

And finally, that unless the bastion to be breached be retrenched on the first and second days of the siege, before the ricochet and vertical fire of 20 heavy pieces with a large quantity of ammunition begin to play upon it, which early retrenchment is not likely, for the enemy cannot correctly know until the opening of the breaching-battery either the mode of attack nor the part to be breached, it would, on the last day, be too late to effect such a retrenchment under a direct fire of 50 24-pounders and a ricochet and vertical one of 16 pieces. The breach being thus open, it surely is not too much to infer from what has been already said, that the troops would not only establish themselves upon it, and circulate round the ramparts, but cause the surrender of the place. At the time of the assault, escalade might be attempted on one part of the town, but particularly on the right face of the intervening ravelin.

It is essential to keep in view, in considering this mode of attack, that the following is the increased proportion of ammunition estimated to be fired in a given time above what is usual from heavy brass ordnance—viz.—four times the quantity in breaching; three times in ricochet, and double from the mortars. However, during a regular siege, as the time of the operation would be necessarily increased, and to save a too great expenditure, perhaps 100 rounds per gun and howitzer in the 24 hours in ricochet would be ample, being twice as much as is commonly made use of.

N. B. The lines marked ----- and ..... on the plan denote the 1st enfilade and vertical fire for 48 hours.

The lines ----- are the 16 24-pounders taken away to make up the breaching battery to 50 guns, leaving thereby the dotted lines ..... for the 2d enfilade and vertical fire.

The continued black lines ——— show the fire from the breaching batteries to breach the wall.

Disposition of Ordnance for an Artillery or accelerated Attack of a Fortress with Bastions & Ravelin having a low Counterscarp & dry Ditch.

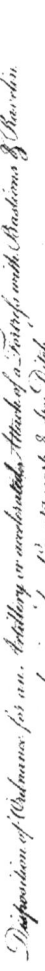

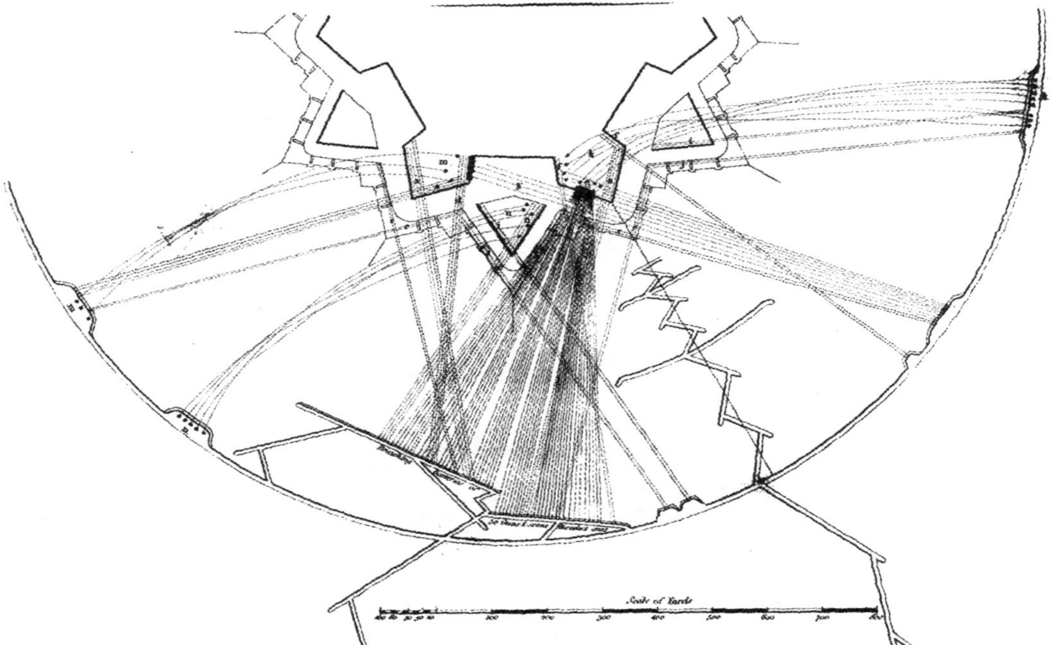

TIME OF THE OPERATION.

Ricochet Batteries ready to receive Ordnance on the 3d Night	2	*days*
Firing from the same 48 Hours until the breach. Battery of 50 Iron 24 Prs be ready & running a boyau as much as possible in advance on the Capital of the Bastion to be breached	2	*do*
Breaching battery armed on the 5th Night, opens the next day and breach assaulted in the evening	1	*do*
If necessary a second days battering	1	*do*
Maximum of Siege	6	*days*

TABLE 1.

Ordnance and Ammunition necessary for an Artillery or Accelerated Siege, with either ONE or TWO Days Battering in Breach, and Three or Four Days Ricochet Firing.

DISPOSITION OF THE ORDNANCE.	Ordnance for First Ricochet, &c.			Ordnance for Second Ricochet and Breaching.			Rounds of Ammunition and Pounds of Powder.										REMARKS.
	24-Pounder, Iron.	68-Pounder Carronade, Iron.	Total of Pieces.	24-Pounder, Iron.	68-Pounder Carronade, Iron.	10-Inch Mortar, Iron.	Total of Pieces.	24-Pounders					68-Pr. Carronade, or 8-Inch Howitzer.			Total 10-Inch Shells.	Total Pounds of Powder.	
								Round Shot.	Spherical Case.	3-Pounder Grape.	Large common Case.	Total for 24-Pounders.	8-Inch common Shell.	Spherical Case.	Common Case.	Total 8-Inch Ammun.			
Bastions and Covered-way — To ricochet the 3 faces of 2 bastions, at 4 guns each face, a. a. a.	12		12																(a) In this estimate of ordnance not a single piece has been given as spare, it not being required, since from what has already been said of the durability of iron ordnance, it is evident none will become unserviceable by its own fire, and only so by being struck by the enemy's shot or shells, which, at the utmost, could not be above two or three pieces; this happening in the ricochet batteries would not be of very material consequence, and in the breaching batteries might be replaced from the ricochet
Do. right face of bastion to be breached, b	2	2	4																
Do. 4 opposite covered-ways of the two bastions, at 2 guns each (c. c. c. c.)	8		8																
Do. flank of bastion looking to the breach, at 4 guns, d.	4		4																
Do. 2 flanks of bastions to be breached, at 2 guns each, l. f.	4		4																
Direct fire of 4 guns to destroy the flank of bastion looking to the bastion breach, g.	4		4																
Ravelins & Covered-way — To ricochet the face of the intermediate ravelin looking to the breach, h.	2	2	4																
Do. right face of the intermediate ravelin and that of the left ravelin, at 2 guns each, i.	4		4																
Do. the opposite covered-ways of the 3 faces of ravelins, at 2 guns each, j.	6		6																
Mortars to play on bastion to be breached, k.						8	8												
Do. on the other bastion, m.						3	3												
Do. on the intermediate ravelin, n.						3	3												
First Ricochet for 48 hours	46	4	16	66				11,040	2,668	92	16	13,800	600	584	16	1,200	3,830	52,072	

Of the above Ordnance may be transferred to the breaching battery—

From the 3 faces of the 2 bastions, 2 guns from each —	6									
From 2 of their opposite covered-ways, at 2 guns each —	4									
From 2 flanks of 2 bastions, at 2 guns each —	4									
From 1 covered-way of intermediate ravelin, at 2 guns	2									
	16									
Add ordnance to complete the breaching-battery to 30 24-pounders, with ammunition for 2 day's breaching	34		500		30,000					
Remaining in battery for second ricochet, &c. with ammunition for 48 hours	30 4 16 50	7,200 1,740	60	9,000	600	584 16	1,200	3,840	44,264
*Maximum of ordnance and ammunition for the siege — (a)	80 4 16 100	47,740 4,408 500 152	52,800	1,200 1,168 32	2,400	7,680	336,336
Deduct ammunition for 1 day's battering and 1 day's ricochet firing —		18,330 870 250 30	19,500	300 292 8	600	1,920	142,132
† Minimum of ammunition for the siege, being 1 day's battering and 3 day's ricochet fire		29,390 3,538 250 122	33,300	900 876 24	1,800	5,760	194,204
Being a Total of Rounds per piece for Maximum, and of lbs. of powder ‡ spare added		597	55 6 2	660	300 292 8	600	480	443,418
Do. do. for Minimum, do. do. —		367	45 3 2	417	225 219 6	440	360	258,938

Number of pieces should be given as spare, since they ruin themselves by their own fire, consequently must, if in any numbers, be replaced.

{ The ammunition required for this siege would therefore be only this quantity with 100 pieces of cannon and for one day's battering.

For *ricochet*, each 24-pounder to fire 150 rounds in the 24 hours; of which 120 to be round shot, 29 spherical case, and 1 large common case. The charges for the round shot to be from 12 to 16 oz., that for spherical case ½; for common case ¾; and for bursting shells 1 lb.

For *battering*, the 24-pounders may fire 300 rounds during day-light, of which 295 round shot and 5 3-pounder grape shot, the latter (in case of necessity) to fire on the breach at night, to prevent clearing or retrenching it, or on the same and ravelin, just before the troops assault. Charge ⅓.

For 68-pounder *carronades*, 150 rounds in the 24 hours, of which 75 to be common 8-inch shells, 73 spherical case, and 2 large common case. Charges from 3 to 5 lbs. of powder; and for bursting shell, common at 2 lbs., and spherical case 1 lb.

For 10-inch *mortars*, 120 common shells in the 24 hours. Charges for and bursting shells, calculated at 6 lbs. per shell.

So few howitzers or carronades are given in the proportion of ordnance, and so many 24-pounders, since the latter answers the double purpose of throwing shot or shells in ricochet, and can be employed in battering from a distance, which the howitzer or carronade cannot.

The 68-pounder carronade on a travelling carriage has been preferred to an 8-inch brass howitzer of the same calibre, it being a longer and better piece of ordnance. The present howitzers are too light and short. Since writing this, there has been constructed at Woolwich, and cast of iron, some excellent 8 and 10-inch howitzers, of six calibres in length; which 8-inch howitzers therefore it would be well to substitute for the 68-pounder carronades before recommended.

* It is evident the above would not be a sufficiency of ammunition for a *regular siege*, which for each 24-pounder should be from 1,200 to 1,500 rounds per gun, 1,000 per howitzer, and 800 per mortar: therefore should such a train be embarked which, with the addition of some pierriers and small mortars, would be a sufficient proportion of ordnance for the operation. In case the place to be besieged be not precisely known, it would be prudent to embark this extra ordnance and ammunition, which would remain on board ship, if not wanted.—*Note.* The ammunition estimated for an artillery siege, is three times more than usually given for enfilades with guns and howitzers; twice more than for mortars; and four times more than employed with brass ordnance to batter in breach.

† The minimum of ordnance for such a siege should not be less than 90 pieces, of which 46 guns, 4 carronades and 16 mortars, or 66 pieces, as above, may be employed for the first 48 hours in ricochet, &c.; and 20 guns, 4 carronades and 16 10-inch mortars, or 90 pieces, may be for the second: thus making a total of 50 24-pounders, 20 24-pounders, 4 carronades and 16 mortars for breaching, 20 24-pounders, 4 carronades and 16 mortars for second ricochet, &c.—being 70 24-pounders, 4 carronades, and 16 10-inch mortars, or 90 pieces of cannon.

‡ In these totals of ammunition one-third of the powder is added as spare.

TABLE II.

PROOF TRIAL WITH FOUR IRON 24-POUNDER GUNS,

Carried on in the Royal Arsenal by the Inspector of Artillery, in pursuance of the Master General's Orders of the 9th September, 1813, and 6th October, 1813, to ascertain what Number of Rounds Iron Ordnance may be capable of sustaining without Injury, where the Fire is incessant.

Description of the Guns: 24-Pounders, 9 feet, cast by

Messrs. Walkers' { Cut No. 238 / Cut No. 80953 } W. Co. 48 0 4 Common Vents.
Carron Company { Cut No. 80807 / Cut No. 81002 } Cwt. qr. lb. 48 2 4 Common Vents. 48 1 12 Wrought Iron Vent. 48 1 18 Copper Vent.

Fired 20th, 21st, and 22d September, marked in First Column, 1st, 2d, 3d days.
Fired 11th, 12th, and 13th October.

The full service Charge was used, viz. { 8 pounds of powder in a paper cartridge with flannel bottom, 1 24-pounder round shot, 2 24-pounder junk wads. }

TRIAL	Days	Rounds No.	TIME			VENTS ENLARGED.							THERMOMETER.					
			Between each Round. Minutes.	In firing the Rounds. Minutes.	For Examination. Minutes.	Messrs. Walkers' Gun. Common Vent.		Carron Company's Guns.					21st, 22d, and 23d September.		11th, 12th, and 13th October.		In the Gun.	
								Common Vent.		Wrought Iron Vent.		Copper Vent.						
						Top.	Bottom.	Top.	Bottom.	Top.	Bottom.	Top.	Bottom.	In the Air. Degrees.	In the Gun. Degrees.	In the Air. Degrees.	In the Gun. Degrees.		
First		25	4	96	24	·004	·003	·003	·005					64	71	53	58		
		25	4	96	11¼	·063	·035	·038	·018	} Increase barely perceptible.		} Increase not perceptible.		67	79	55	66		
		25	4	96	24	·068	·046	·043	·033					68	78	58	63		
		25	4	96	End of the Firing.	·078	·063	·048	·038					60	71	56	64		
Second		50	3	147	24	·103	·078	·073	·05	·033	·011	ditto.	ditto.	68	83	56	64		
		50	3	147	72	·105	·088	·078	·058	·048	·02	·003	"	62	92	56	72		
		50	3	147	End of the Firing.	·113	·108	·103	·077	·053	·02	·020	·008	62	90	58	87		
Third		50	3	147	24	·163	·113	·128	·078	·088	·028	·028	·01	66	83	58	78		
		50	3	147	72	·218	·178	·135	·118	·098	·03	·03	·013	66	92	56	72		
		50	3	147	End of the Firing.	·25	·203	·178	·123	·138	·093	·033	·017	62	89	55	72		

After firing 400 Rounds from each of the Guns with Iron Vents, on the 20th, 21st, and 22d September, their Bores were carefully examined and found not in the least injured, except being a little dented near the seat of the shot, and notwithstanding the Vents continued to enlarge, yet that of Wrought Iron in so small a degree as to afford a prospect of very considerable resistance; from which, on the Report on this subject, of the above dates, it was recommended that Iron Ordnance demanded for Siege might be vented previous to their being issued, as also that spare Vents should be sent to replace such as may be damaged by long and severe service: but from the favourable result of the subsequent trial on the 11th, 12th, and 13th October, carried on by the approval of the Master General, with a Gun of the same description, vented with pure Copper, appears that a decided preference should be given to it, unless for the better determining the point (especially as to the agreement of the two metals, Copper or Iron, when in contact) it might be advisable, should Battering Ordnance be demanded, to send a proportion vented in each way.

TABLE III.

RETURN OF ORDNANCE AND EXPENDITURE OF AMMUNITION AT THE SIEGES OF CIUDAD RODRIGO AND BADAJOZ, IN 1812, AND ST. SEBASTIAN, IN 1813.

PLACES	Ordnance: 24-Pdr Iron	18-Pdr Iron	8-In. Howitzer Brass	68-Pdr Carronade Iron	5½-Inch Howitzer Iron	10-Inch Mortar Iron	Total of Pieces	24-Pdr: Round Shot	Grape and Case	Spherical Case Shot	Total 24-Pounder	18-Pdr: Round	Grape and Case	Spherical Case Shot	Total 18-Pounder	8-In. How. & 68-Pdr Carr.: Common Shells	Spherical Case Shot	Total 8-In. Ammunition	5½-In. How.: Common Shells	Spherical Case Shot	Total 5½-Inch	10-Inch Mortar	General Total Rounds	Total Pounds of Powder	Rounds per Piece: 24-Pr. and 5½-In. How.	18-Pounder	8-In. Howitzer & 68-Pr. Car.	5½-Inch Howitzer	10-Inch Mortar
At Ciudad Rodrigo	34	4	—	—	—	—	38	8,950	—	—	8,950	565	—	—	565	—	—	—	—	—	—	—	9,515	182,489	263	141	—	—	—
Badajoz, in 1812	16/20	—	—	—	16	—	52	18,832	1,163	—	19,995	13,029	496	—	13,525	—	—	—	507	1,319	1,826	—	35,346	227,070	*1,249	676	—	114	—
St. Sebastian, the First and Second Sieges	48	6/13	8	—	20	—	†95	45,367	2,094	1,930	47,391	9,303	—	150	9,453	7,766	2,198	9,964	—	—	—	3,755	70,563	502,110	987	1,575	474	—	188

* Much of this 24-pounder round shot was used by the 24-pounder or 5½-inch iron howitzer in enfilade.

† At *First Siege* only employed on the Right, 20 24-pounders, 6 8-inch howitzers, 4 68-pounder carronades, and 4 10-inch mortars:—on Left attack, 6 18-pounders. At *Second Siege*, on Right and Left, 95 pieces of ordnance.

Plate II

Appearance which the Bottoms of the Vents or Surfaces of the Metal surrounding them made in the Box at each period of examination by three 24 Pounders fired from rest by the undermentioned Founderies.

When examined	CARRON COMPANY		MESS.RS WALKERS
	Wrought Iron Vent	Common Vent	Common Vent
1813. 20.th Sept.r after the Days firing. 150 Rounds.	(small shape)	(shape)	(shape)
21.st September 1813. After the first 50 Rounds.	(shape)	(shape)	(shape)
After the second 50 Rounds.	(shape)	(shape)	(shape)

After the
third 50
Rounds.

After the
first 50
Rounds.

After the
second 50
Rounds.

After the
third 50
Rounds.

22nd September 1813.

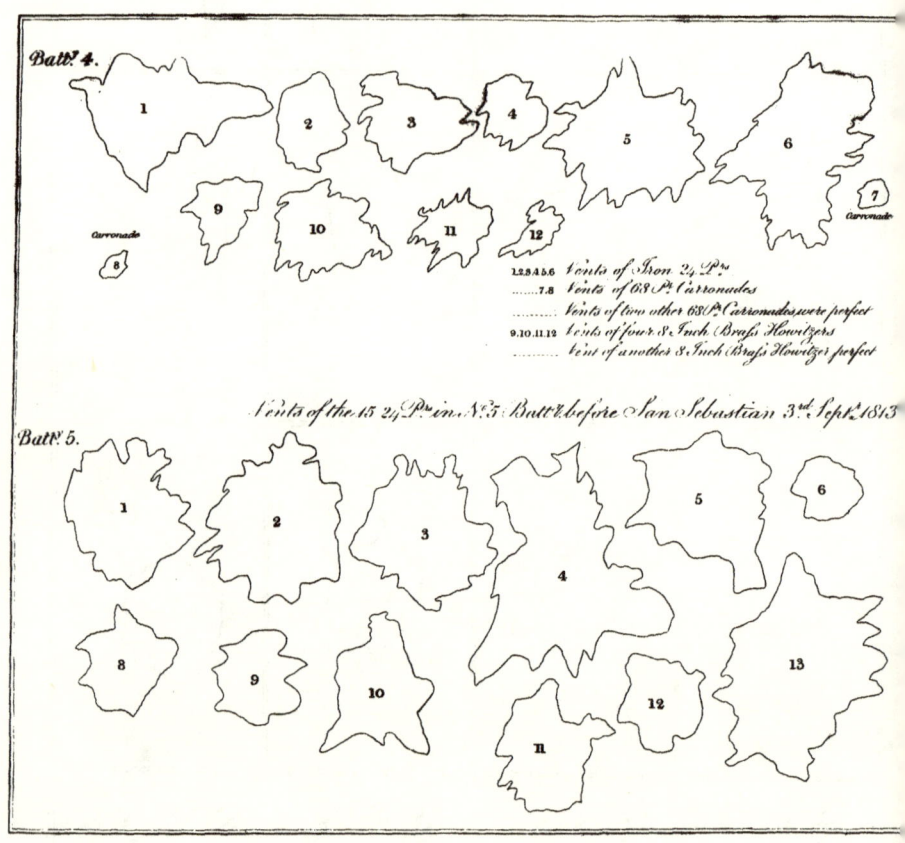

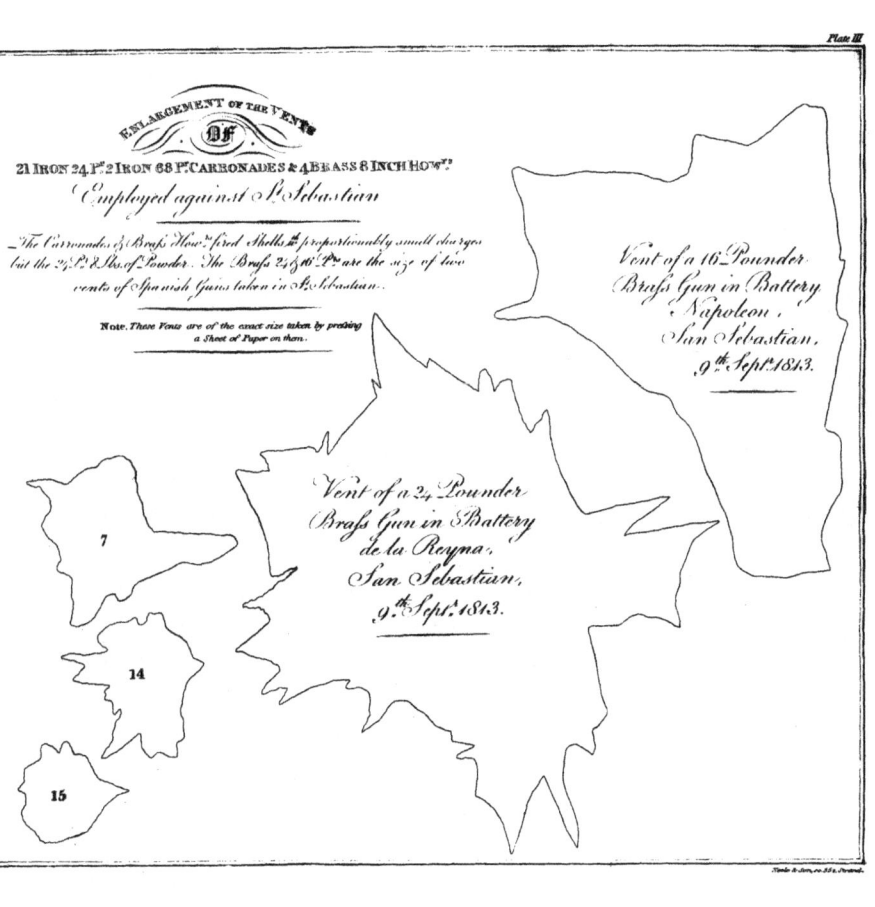

NOTES.

NOTE (A.)

THE calibre of a Russian 18-pounder is 5·45 inches in diameter, that of an English one 5·29, the English shot being 5·04, the Russian gun gave a windage of ·41, while the English is only ·25 with its own shot. Dr. Hutton, in his experiments of Artillery, states, " That a very great increase of velocity arises from a decrease of windage, it appearing that with the established windage of $\frac{1}{20}$ between $\frac{1}{3}$ and $\frac{1}{4}$ of the force is lost." As therefore the English shot in the Russian guns gave a windage of about $\frac{4}{10}$ of an inch; it is apparent that English 18-pounders with their proper shot would have battered with much more effect than Russian guns with English shot.

On account of the difference of windage, at the end of the siege the vents of the Russian guns were scarcely affected by the firing, whereas those of the English 24-pounders were extremely enlarged, though the bores of the 24-pounders remained perfect.

NOTE (B.)

This conclusion is not exactly correct, for it is obvious that 50 guns would make a breach in proportion quicker in one day, than 20 of the same calibre in $2\frac{1}{2}$ days; for let us suppose the difference of weight of 20 24-pounder shot, or 50 24-pounder shot striking a wall at the same moment, not only would *each individual shot* from 50 guns damage the wall equally with that from the 20 guns, but the momentum would be greater from the 50 than from the 20, according to the difference of weight, or, in other words, the rampart would be less shook by 20 than by 50 shots; as in ancient times, the larger battering-ram destroyed a wall quicker than a smaller one. This argument is also in favour of firing salvos from the breaching batteries, provided the guns be nearly as quickly served.

NOTE (C.)

Dr. Hutton on this subject says, " That velocities arising from firing with different quantities of powder, are nearly in the proportion of the square roots of the quantities or weights of powder."

Thus the 24-pounders charged with 8 lbs. and others with 6 lbs. their relative effects will be as 2·828 is to 2·449; that is to say, 43 24-pounders with the larger charge, should do nearly as much as 50 24-pounders with the smaller one.

NOTE (D.)

Lieut.-Colonel Jones, in his Journal, speaking of the damage done to, and inefficiency of, brass ordnance, at the siege of Badajoz, in May and June, 1811, says,—

Page 58.—" The number of brass pieces of ordnance brought to the second siege, were, 26 24-pounders, 8

16-pounders, 2 8-inch and 4 10-inch howitzers, being 40 pieces for the two attacks."

Page 65.—" The Portugueze guns proved of a very soft nature, and could not stand the present heavy firing, 12 pieces of ordnance only were now serviceable at this attack, (St. Christoval,) and kept up a continued fire, but with little effect."

Page 71.—" The materiel of the artillery employed was excessively bad, and totally inadequate to the undertaking, although every thing Elvas could supply was drawn from thence; the guns were of a soft composition of metal, false in their bore, &c. The shot were of all shapes and sizes, giving a windage from 1-tenth to half an inch. The howitzers used as mortars were of little service, they were not steady on their beds, the shells did not fit them; the practice was therefore necessarily vague and uncertain, and considerable credit is due to the officers of artillery for having effected so much with such crude materials and under such disadvantageous circumstances. After the failure of the second assault of the breach of St. Christoval, no hope could be entertained of the reduction of the place, as the shot collected for the siege were nearly expended, and Elvas could supply no more: 18 pieces had been disabled (by their own fire), and there were no others to replace them."

NOTE (E.)

Several of these *iron* 24-pounders were bouched with copper by order of Lieut.-Colonel Sir Alexander Dickson, (who commanded the artillery at these sieges with infinite credit to himself and benefit to the service,) and left in an excellent state at Elvas; the same operation was performed with 23 iron 24-pounders afterwards given over to the Spaniards at St. Sebastian and formed the chief armament of the place.

All the *brass* ordnance taken in St. Sebastian, (see Plate III. of the size of vents of a Spanish brass 24 and 16-pounders,) were utterly incapable of any farther service, both as to the vents and enlargement of the bores, though it is evident these *brass* guns could not have been put to the same severe trials as the *iron* ones used for battering.

NOTE (F.)

Count de la Martillière, in his work entitled " Réflexions sur la fabrication en général des bouches à feu," edition of 1796, says, No. 36: " A l'époque des dernières guerres de Flandres," (ending in 1748,) "les poudres étoient reçues dans les magasins à 60 toises de portée: actuellement (1796) non seulement l'ordonnance en exige 100, mais elles portent presque toutes à 120, et quelques-unes jusqu'à 130 toises: l'agent destructif des bouches à feu ayant donc presque doublé de force, il n'est pas étonnant que les pièces de 16 et de 24 (of brass) qui soient soumises à ce nouvel agent, ne résistent pas autant que lorsqu'elles n'avoient affaire qu'à *un agent moitié* moins fort."

NOTE (G.)

See *Gay de Vernon's Traité de l'Art Militaire,* vol. i. page 84. published in 1805, wherein he considers the cast iron ordnance as inferior to brass; and would recommend the forged iron guns but for the difficulty and expence of its manufacture.

See also *Monge sur l'Art de fabriquer les Canons,* p.41.

" Comme la ténacité du fer coulé est 5 à 6 fois moindre que celle du fer forgé, on est obligé de donner aux pièces de même calibre, des dimensions beaucoup plus fortes qu'on ne ferait si elles étoient en fer forgé; ce qui charge les batiments de mer d'un poid inutile.—On a lieu d'espérer que le zèle des républicains, et les connoissances en tout genre qu'il est temps enfin de rendre populaires, nous mettront incessamment en état de surmonter toutes les difficultés qui jusqu'ici ont retardé l'emploi du *fer forgé* pour la fabrication des pièces de grosse artillerie, tant pour le service de la marine, que pour celui de la guerre de terre."

NOTE (H.)

To shew how perfectly inefficient brass *battering* ordnance is even to this day with the French, the reader is referred again to Comte de la Martillière, (editions of 1796 and 1817.)—He principally treats of some experiments made in 1786 at Douai, by order of the French Minister at War, to ascertain the durability of *brass ordnance,* cast by two founders, with different alloys of copper and tin.—The pieces of brass ordnance tried were 29, which consisted of 10 heavy guns, 16 and 24-pounders; 13 field-pieces, 4, 8, and 12-pounders; and 6, 8, and 12-inch mortars; when the following *average* number of rounds were fired from each (with the exception of the mortars) before they were rendered perfectly unserviceable :—

Ordnance.	Rounds.
5 4-pounders	2,419
4 8————	3,000
4 12————	1,553
6 16————	982
4 24————	92
4 8-inch mortars	600
2 12————	600

The trunnions of the mortars were not strong enough, and were found to be giving way, so that the experiment as to them was not pushed to the utmost.—One of the 6 16-pounders fired 3,400 rounds before it was rendered completely unserviceable, which circumstance is not accounted for, since the other 5 pieces did not average more than 623 rounds, of which one 16-pounder was rendered useless after 50 rounds.—One of the 5 4-pounders would only stand 596 rounds, whereas there were fired from each of the other four, 3,000 rounds; the first La Martillière accounts for by saying, it was so soon rendered unserviceable by the gun being loaded with a *loose* shot, without the shot, as is customary in field-service, being fixed to a wood bottom, or by the same means to a cartridge. In the experiments with the 16 and 24-pounders, it is singular, considering the above remark, that the committee of officers should not have tried the durability of these pieces, particularly the 24-pounders, by practising with shot fixed to wood-bottoms, instead of without them; in 3 out of 4 of the 24-pounders one great reason why they were so promptly destroyed was from shot breaking in them.

Though the experiments quoted as to the damage done to the bores be extremely minute and satisfactory, yet in no case, except one, is the slightest mention made as to the vents of the guns, which, when the number of rounds fired was great, must have suffered proportionately with the bores, which was seen by brass cannon taken in Badajoz and St. Sebastian, &c.

No. 38.—" Les trois officiers généraux, (MM. Le Marquis de Thiboutot, le Chevalier de Gomer et Désalmont) qui présidoient à ces épreuves, avant de se séparer, dressèrent, d'après les instructions du ministre, un procès-verbal de leurs opinions, motivées sur les résultats de ces épreuves extraordinaires et comparatives, qui certifioient à l'unanimité, que le service *des trois calibres de campagne étoit très assuré, et pour la durée de plusieurs actions vives et consécutives et au-delà de toute crainte :* mais que celui *des pièces de siège et de place (16 et de 24) étoit, à leur grand étonnement, très incertain pour la durée de celui auquel elles sont exclusivement destinées.—* D'après ce rapport franc et loyal, la fabrication des pièces de 24 et de 16 fut suspendue jusqu'à nouvel ordre par ordre du ministre."

No. 43.—" Depuis cette époque, l'expérience ayant malheureusement de plus en plus convaincu les artilleurs de l'insuffisance des pièces de *gros calibre*, par leur trop courte durée dans les actions et les sièges que nos diverses armées ont eu à soutenir, surtout en Espagne dans les années de 1793, 1794 et 1795, par les plus graves inconvéniens éprouvés à raison des fréquens recharges que cette artillerie, si promptement mise hors de service, nécessitoit au grand mécontentement de l'armée, qu'ils accabloient de fatigue, ayant à transporter à bras d'homme ces grosses pièces sur des montagnes, d'un accès très escarpé, et avant nous inaccessibles à cette grosse artillerie, dans les sièges de St. Elme, de la citadelle de Roses et du château de la Trinité, (Bouton de Rose)—"

No. 44.—" Ce qui étoit arrivé à l'armée des Pyrénées orientales arriva quelques années après à l'armée du Rhin et Moselle, commandée par le Général Moreau ; à la défense mémorable des têtes-de-pont de Kehl et de Huningue contre le Prince Charles ; des plaintes furent portées au ministre de la guerre par le Général Eblé, commandant alors l'artillerie de cette armée."

No. 45.—" Le Ministre d'alors, le Général Scherer, désirant prendre ces plaintes en grande considération, fut supplié par le commissaire de la fonderie royale de Strasbourg, de se faire représenter le résultat des épreuves extraordinaires de Douai in 1786 ; et comme le ministre ne donna pas suite à cette affaire, il est à présumer qu'il trouva dans ces procès-verbaux, de justes motifs pour ne pas donner cours à cette plainte quoique bien fondée de la part du Général Eblé."

La Martillière states, for reasons given, that *brass* ordnance, instead of being brought to greater perfection, like other mechanical arts, at the present day, is much inferior to what it was at the beginning of the 18th century.

But though, as he conceives, alloying gun metal with zinc might give it rather more resistance, and perhaps the old mode of casting which he recommends, yet as nothing new or very efficient is pointed out whereby the larger calibre of *brass* ordnance for sieges can be founded of such strength as to be equal to the service required, the substitution of *heavy iron ordnance* is indispensably necessary.

The author, however, goes on to recommend the re-casting of a quantity of heavy *brass* ordnance, in what he considers an ameliorated state, for the larger calibres; and finishes his book by timid remarks as to *iron ordnance*, by which it is apparent he has not sufficient confidence in its goodness fully to recommend it for sieges; since, undoubtedly, it has not arrived at that point of perfection in France at which the British ordnance of that nature now stands.

NOTE (I).

In consequence of the enlargement of the vents of the *iron* guns at the sieges of Badajoz and St. Sebastian, Lord Mulgrave, then Master-General of the Ordnance, gave orders in September and October, 1813, for trials with 4 24-pounders to ascertain " what number of rounds (this) iron ordnance was capable of sustaining without injury when the fire is incessant."—2 of the 24-pounders had common vents, the 3d a wrought iron one, and the

4th one of copper. *In three days* 400 rounds were fired from each, and the result appears to be, that the copper vents resisted the best, and were scarcely at all enlarged, that of wrought iron afforded considerable resistance, but the common vents were greatly encreased in size; the bores of the pieces were not in the least injured, except by the smallest indenture possible at the seat of the shot, (see the detail of these experiments, page 54, and Plate II.)—These trials as far as they go are useful, but, to be eminently so, they should have been pushed much farther, to from 2 to 3,000 rounds a gun, and at the rate of 500 rounds in the 24 hours fired from each, not only to decide most fully the point, the metal of most resistance with which iron guns for siege and garrison should be bouched, but to show in what degree the cylinders of the pieces would be injured, and consequently how far it was likely to affect their accuracy in striking the object.

As before stated (see Note E.) 23 of the iron 24-pounders were rebouched, and left in the fortress of St. Sebastian, but 15 out of the whole of the 24-pounders most damaged by the firing (9 and $9\frac{1}{2}$ feet guns) were sent to Woolwich and regularly examined at the proof-house; the state of their vents may be seen by those of the 21 24-pounders shown in plate, No. III, at the end of this work; the damage, however, sustained in the bores of the 15 pieces was found to be so inconsiderable, that had their vents stood, the guns, no doubt, might have been employed and serviceable for one or two more sieges; it was ascertained that in no case was there a graze caused by the shot in its passage through the cylinder of more than $\frac{1}{20}$th of an inch in depth, and at the seat of the shot, where is always the greatest injury, in 5 of the 24-pounders, there were only dents of $\frac{3}{40}$th of an inch, and in the other 10 pieces not more than $\frac{1}{20}$th of the same, and that, generally speaking, the injury sustained was at the seat of the shot and two or three feet before it, the cylinders near the muzzle of the pieces being scarcely at all indented.

At the first part of the siege of St. Sebastian, 20 24-pounders were used in battering, six of which belonged to the Surveillante frigate and were returned on board her, therefore only 14 out of the 15 24-pounders examined at Woolwich, it is probable, were among the latter guns. As these 15 guns appear to have been selected from among the most damaged, it is likely that 14 of them were the 24-pounders made use of in the two attacks.

Now as, at the first part of this siege, these guns were employed four days in battering in breach, and at the second part, from the 26th to the 30th of August inclusive, being five days more, thus making a total of nine days, which, at 300 rounds a day per gun, would give 2,700 rounds for each of the 14 24-pounders, it is evident that the damage sustained in the cylinders of these pieces is extremely insignificant and of no account in proportion to their use. We will even take it at the lowest rate by supposing that the 14 guns were only used at the first attack; this would make 1,200 fired per gun, and by supposing the damaged guns taken from those only employed at the second attack, the guns in that case would have fired 1,500 rounds per gun.—See Plate III., wherein is given the degrees of damage done to the vents of 21 iron 24-pounders, 2 iron 68-pounder carronades, and 4 *brass* 8-inch howitzers. In the same plate will be seen (as before-mentioned) the immense enlargement of the vents of a 24 and 16-pounder *brass* guns employed by the garrison. It is very singular that in besieging St. Sebastian the vents of 4 brass 8-inch howitzers, Nos. 9, 10, 11, and 12, (see the plate,) that were bushed with *copper*, should have been infinitely more enlarged than the vents of 2 *iron* 68-pounder carronades, (of the same bore and charged with a similar quantity of powder and equally fired,) Nos. 7 and 8, which iron vents were perforated through their own metal. The very enlarged vents of the *brass* Spanish 16 and 24-pounders it is probable were originally of copper.

If so, this would appear to militate against the conclusion drawn from the Woolwich experiments, as to the superiority of the copper to the wrought-iron vents.

The 24-pounders employed at the last siege against Badajoz were all left at Elvas, on account of the difficulty of their transport to Lisbon.

May not the damage done to the cylinders, but particularly to the vents of brass and iron ordnance, by the action of fired gun-powder, be accounted for, in a great measure, on the principle of the blow-pipe used in chemistry? We know the blow-pipe to be a small tube impelling, by means of the breath or bellows, a column of air through flame, by which metals are fused, in consequence of the rapidity and quick succession of the flame consuming the oxygen of the common air, and causing thereby an intense heat, similar to a draft of air forced through a furnace by bellows or otherwise.

Robins, in his Gunnery, (Edit. 1805, p. 71.) says, "That the heat of powder, when fired in any considerable quantity, is not less than that of red-hot iron."— And, in the next page, "Hence the absolute quantity of the pressure exerted by gunpowder at the moment of its explosion may be assigned, for, since the fluid then generated has an elasticity of $999\frac{1}{3}$," (Dr. Hutton, in a note, says, near 1600 times,) "or in round numbers, 1,000 times greater than common air, and since common air, by its elasticity, exerts a pressure on any given surface equal to the weight of the incumbent atmosphere with which it is in equilibrio; the pressure exerted by fired gunpowder, before it has dilated itself, is nearly 1,000 times greater than the pressure of the atmosphere, and, consequently, the quantity of this force on the surface of a square inch amounts to about six ton weight, which force, however, diminishes as the fluid dilates itself. Thus, as before said, the action of the powder would appear on metals, when fired through cylinders, to have the principle of the blow-pipe in fusing them, for we see the flame generated is not less than a red-heat, and that it is impelled forward and upwards through the vent with infinitely more rapidity than is done through the tube of the blow-pipe by the breath or bellows; so that were this action constant, neither brass nor even iron cannon could withstand its effects; but as it is only partial in proportion to the number of rounds fired, its effects would appear to be according to the quantity of powder, and the fusibility of the metals its influence is exerted upon, taking especially into consideration, that through so small a tube as a vent, the injury sustained will be comparatively greater than through the cylinder of the piece.

In Dr. Gregory's Dictionary of Arts and Sciences, the properties of the metals in question are stated as follows :—

" The metal of brass cannon is composed of from 6 to 12 parts of tin combined with 100 parts of copper, this alloy is brittle, yellow, heavier than copper, and has more tenacity, it is *much more fusible,* and less liable to be altered by the exposure to the air." " *Tin,* next to lead, is the softest and least elastic of all the metals, in tenacity it is superior only to lead: except cast iron, it is the lightest of all the metals."

Iron—" Is the hardest and most elastic of the metals : its tenacity is such, that an iron wire of 0·078 of an inch in diameter is capable of supporting 549·25 lbs. averdupois, without breaking : it is very difficult to fuze."

Now from the same authority we find the points of fusion of these and two other metals to be :—

That Tin melts at 442° of Farenheit's.
        Lead . . 594° of ditto.
        Zinc . . 700° of ditto.
        Copper . . . . . . 27° of Wedgewood.
        Iron . . . . 158° of ditto.

Therefore when it be found that the brass guns, particularly those of the larger calibres, in rapid firing droop at the muzzle, and in the bore lose their regular cylindric form, must we not attribute this, in a great measure, to the action of the powder melting and separating part of the tin, (which is so extremely fusible,) and leaving thereby the copper, which being softened by the heat, is more or less damaged by the action of the shot passing along the cylinder in leaving the piece, which injury will, in a great measure, be according to the degree of heat generated and the quickness of the firing.

But as iron requires such an intense heat to fuze it, and therefore is not softened by that caused by the quickest firing, so that the shot in passing through the cylinder will alter its form, the piece must retain the necessary accuracy in striking the object, though from the practice at the sieges detailed, and the reasons already given, the vents were found to be greatly damaged by the intense heat therein generated. The result of the above reasoning, but particularly the experience at the sieges, evidently show, that the iron ordnance is infinitely superior to the brass in the larger or even smaller calibres for siege, garrison, or field-service.

Antoni on Artillery, chap. viii. recommends forged iron as the only one that can be depended on for making screw bouches, which bouches, he says, may, in case of damage, be removed and replaced by spare ones in a few minutes, and performed in the batteries without dismounting the guns. His remarks were meant to apply to brass ordnance, but they are even more just as to the iron ones.

NOTE (K.)

It has been suggested, that when the height of the counterscarp from the bottom of the dry ditch be more than from 10 to 12 feet, that the difficulty might be overcome by mechanical means, instead of bags filled with wool or hay, and short ladders, as used at Ciudad Rodrigo and Badajoz; but though the mechanical means in question might with ease be resorted to, yet the author does not bring it forward as necessary to the low counterscarp he has mentioned in this attack; but as the depth of the ditch may not always be precisely known, since the idea is very simple and useful in itself, it ought not to be passed over in silence :

It consists in having a quantity of very thick plank, of about 20 or 25 feet long, from 2 to 4 of which should be placed side by side and battened strongly together, then balanced over a temporary axletree and nailed to it, wheels for which axletree might be taken from the trench carts; slips of wood should be nailed, at short distances, on the breadth of the boards to prevent the foot slipping in running down them; four sappers might with ease run such a bridge forward, shoot it over the counterscarp just before the troops were going to the assault, which bridge having, at the nearest end, a rope attached, should be made fast to a palisade or picket post.

Thus, by constructing as many of these bridges as were equal to the length of the breach or the front of the storming party, and placing the bridges together, an inclined plane would be formed to facilitate the passage of the troops into the ditch, their order thereby being kept more entire than if they leapt into it.

NOTE (L.)

With an *engine* so overwhelming, powerful, and accurate, as a battery of 50 iron 24-pounders, it is difficult to say what may not be achieved, by directing its fire to a *focus* against a fortress, particularly in the case where the rampart is seen much above the glacis, and from the lowness of the ground round the place the ricochet-batteries cannot have their full effect to dismount the enemy's artillery: there would appear no great difficulty with such a battery to cut the work down below the cordon, and lay bare their artillery, from whence the besiegers are galled by the enemy's fire, and that the ricochet one cannot subdue.

NOTE (M.)

The navy, when engaged at close quarters with an enemy's ship, are in the habits of firing with one charge two round shot, or one round and one grape shot from iron guns; the iron ordnance undergoes accordingly a severe proof to ensure its standing such trials on service. Why therefore might not this practice on land be useful in the case of a *regular* siege, where the work be battered in breach from the *crest of the glacis*, decreasing the charge from $\frac{1}{3}$d to $\frac{1}{4}$th. i. e. for a 24-pounder using 6 lbs. instead of 8? It has been found that two round shot from one charge range very accurately together for even more than double the distance that would be required in this case. As the ground on the crest of a glacis is confined, and will only allow a very few guns to be placed there to batter the work, and it being essential it should be breached rapidly, it may be fairly inferred, with the decreased charge the advantage gained by the use each time of 2 round shot would at *least* be equal to an addition of two-thirds more guns, i. e. 12 guns with 2 shot would be equal to 20 with 1 shot.

This remark, as it only applies to a *regular* siege, may perhaps be considered as irrelevant, but since it might be useful, it was not thought proper to omit it.

THE END.

www.ingramcontent.com/pod-product-compliance
Lightning Source LLC
Chambersburg PA
CBHW032010080426
42735CB00007B/553